A. Leonard Meyer

Meyer's Business Directory of the City of Phoenix, Arizona

A. Leonard Meyer

Meyer's Business Directory of the City of Phoenix, Arizona

ISBN/EAN: 9783744693912

Printed in Europe, USA, Canada, Australia, Japan

Cover: Foto ©Andreas Hilbeck / pixelio.de

More available books at **www.hansebooks.com**

MEYER'S
BUSINESS DIRECTORY

OF THE CITY OF

PHŒNIX, ARIZONA.

CONTAINING A

Classified Business and Professional Guide; a List of all the City and County and Federal Officials; Correct Tables of Railroad Fares, Express Tariffs and Telegraph Tolls to All Points of the Compass,

AND OTHER VALUABLE INFORMATION.

COMPILED AND PUBLISHED BY

A. LEONARD MEYER,

PHŒNIX, ARIZONA,

1888.

Copyrighted.)

THE CITY OF PHŒNIX.

* Embowered in the mass of verdant foliage, which line every street and surround every dwelling-place, adorned by a wealth of flowers and shrubbery, and with beautiful gardens, vineyards and orchards about every suburban home, Phœnix can justly boast of being one of the handsomest little cities on the Pacific Slope. Through every street streams of pure, clear water are conducted along the edge of the sidewalks, cooling the atmosphere during the summer months, and bringing life and verdure and productiveness to flowers and fruits and shade trees. The ground upon which the town is built has a gradual slope toward the Salt river, distant about one mile. The original town-site embraces one-half section—a mile in length by a half-mile in width. To this, however, have been added during the past year more than a dozen additions. Situated very near the center of the great valley, and about thirty-five miles north of Maricopa station, on the Southern Pacific Railroad, the site of the city is everything that could be desired. The facilities for drainage toward the river are perfect, as are also those for the establishment of a comprehensive water supply system. The important question of sanitation is therefore settled for all time, and the healthfulness of the city assured. The grading and paving of streets, and the construction of sidewalks will be here an easy task, and the cost reduced to a minimum owing to the level contour of the surface.

THE BUILDINGS,

Public and private, of this rapidly-growing young city, are creditable to the enterprise of its people. The old adobe of the early pioneer is fast disappearing before the march of progress. The streets cross each other at right angles, and there are three plazas, or public squares. In one of these the county court-house stands, a commodious brick structure of two stories, crowned by a handsome clock tower. The other plaza will soon be occupied by a city hall. It will be of brick and stone, two stories in height. Adorned with shrubbery, grass and shade trees, these squares will be an attractive feature of the town.

The public school-house is a roomy and comfortable edifice of brick, and accommodates at present over 500 pupils. But so rapid is the increase in population that the school trustees have decided to erect at once three

——*The following sketch is from the facile pen of Hon. Patrick Hamilton, recently published in the Albuquerque *Democrat*, with such minor changes as the march of progress have made necessary.

C. Eschman & Co.

APOTHECARIES

N. W. Corner

Center and Washington Streets,

PHŒNIX, A. T.

A FULL LINE OF ALL CLASSES OF GOODS
USUALLY FOUND IN A FIRST-CLASS

DRUG STORE.

PRESCRIPTIONS CAREFULLY PREPARED, Day or Night.

more school buildings, which will give the city four public schools, or one to each ward.

Washington street, which runs from east to west through the center of the city, is the main business thoroughfare. A mile in length—exclusive of additions—and 120 feet in width, it can boast of many handsome mercantile establishments. These are mostly of brick, many of them carrying immense stocks and doing a volume of business, running into the hundreds of thousands annually, besides supplying the immense valley, of which it is the center. The trade of Phœnix embraces all the mining camps and cattle ranges within a radius of seventy-five miles.

Already the young city is supplied with many churches, nearly all the leading Christian sects being represented. Catholics, Methodists, (north and south) Presbyterians, Baptists, Episcopalians and Congregationalists, have places of worship, the Catholic and Methodist churches being commodious edifices. The secret orders are prosperous here. The Masons, Odd Fellows, Order of United Workmen, Knights of Pythias, Red Men, Chosen Friends and Good Templars, have flourishing lodges. There is a Library Association, supported by popular subscriptions, and a number of social and charitable organizations attached to the several churches. With such a showing for moral and intellectual progress, the charge of "general cussedness" so often heard against the "rowdy west," cannot affect Phœnix.

The newspaper is the truest mirror of a people's moral and material condition. In this respect Phœnix need not fear comparison with more pretentious places. The *Arizonian, Herald* and *Gazette* issue daily and weekly editions, while the *Advance* is published once a week. A perusal of their local and advertising columns will give an outsider an excellent idea of the growth and prosperity of the town and of the enterprise and public spirit of its citizens. That the people of Phœnix appreciate the work of its press is evinced by the liberal support which they extend to it.

THE POPULATION

Of this coming city of the southwest is estimated at 5,000, which is being rapidly augmented since the completion of the branch railroad. Three banks, with a heavy capitalization, are required to meet its steady growing business. There are several hotels, and yet another, a large brick structure, will be finished within two months. There are two manufactories of artificial ice, a large flouring mill, a planing mill and a meat packing establishment near the town. A three-story opera house, is recently com-

THE
NATIONAL BANK of ARIZONA,

PHŒNIX, ARIZONA.

Capital Paid Up, - - $100,000.

DIRECTORS

M. W. KALES,   SOL. LEWIS,   J. Y. T. SMITH,
        CHAS. GOLDMAN,   GEO. W. HOADLEY.

CORRESPONDENTS:

THE BANK OF CALIFORNIA, San Francisco. AGENCY OF BANK OF
CALIFORNIA, New York. Messrs. N. M. ROTHS-
CHILD & SONS, London.

M. W. KALES,   **SOL. LEWIS,**   **GEO. W. HOADLEY,**
President.   *Vice-President.*   *Cashier.*

The VALLEY BANK of PHŒNIX
ARIZONA.

Paid Up Capital, - - $50,000.
Surplus, - - - - 13,000.

OFFICERS:

ANDREW CRAWFORD, President.   WM. CHRISTY, Cashier.
        E. J. BENNITT. Assistant Cashier.

DIRECTORS

A. CRAWFORD,   F. C. HATCH,   M. H. SHERMAN,
        WM. CHRISTY,   E. J. BENNITT.

CORRESPONDENTS: PACIFIC BANK, San Francisco. FIRST NATIONAL
BANK, Los Angeles. AMERICAN EXCHANGE NATIONAL BANK, New York
City. S. A. KEAN & CO., Chicago.

Drafts Drawn on all the Principal Cities of Europe.

pleted. Another hotel of 200 hundred rooms is now projected, and will soon be built. The city is lighted by gas, and will soon have electric light, a company having been organized for that purpose. Street cars traverse the city and several of the additions. There is an excellent fire department, supplied with the latest improved apparatus.

In a word, Phœnix has fairly entered upon the road which leads to prosperity, and is rapidly forging ahead. Her's will be no mushroom growth, no ephemeral "boom." Sustained and supported by the vast tract of rich and productive soil which surrounds it on all sides, with abundance of water and a perfect climate, she can look to the future with serene confidence. She has the unfailing resources which build cities and support prosperous communities. Now that her superb gifts and advantages are becoming known, property values are rapidly rising. The past six months have witnessed many improvements both in the city and suburbs, and prices have fully doubled within that period. There has been no feverish "boom," but a steady advancement, born of confidence in the future. The field for the investor or speculator is an inviting one, and many fortunes will be made in this valley in real estate within the next twelve months. At present there are about fifteen firms engaged in the business, which will give some idea of the transfers made. Lots in this city, which could be had for $150 six months ago, now command $500 and $600, and so it is with suburban tracts and business locations. This year will bring to the valley many visitors from the east and west, and transactions in realty promise to be lively enough to suit the most sanguine "boomer."

"THE GARDEN OF THE SOUTHWEST,"

Is the name which has not been inaptly applied to this vale of beauty and productiveness. Columns might be filled descriptive of the many gifts which generous nature has showered upon it. There is no necessity for the writer to indulge in hyperbole or exaggeration. The plain facts speak louder than any highly painted picture. Only yesterday reclaimed from the desert, its fruitful fields, orchards and vineyards are already a glorious promise of the future. When its hundreds of thousands of untilled acres will smile beneath their burdens of the fruits of every clime; when handsome houses with their wealth, shrubbery and flowers shall adorn the landscape; when the air with its musical feathered songsters and heavy with odors as delicious as those from the isles of the eastern seas, and when over all are the skies of a cloudless clime, then indeed may the visitor exclaim —"if there be an elysium on earth, it is this, it is this."

CITY OF PHŒNIX.

MUNICIPAL DIRECTORY.

De Forest Porter .... Mayor
John R. Loosley . } .... { 1st Ward
Sam'l Franklin .. } Councilmen .... { 2d Ward
Geo. H. Rothrock } .... { 3d Ward
Lincoln Fowler .. } .... { 4th Ward
Frank Baxter..Recorder
A. Leonard Meyer ....Treasurer
Frank D. Wells...Marshal
A. C. Baker ....Attorney
Dr. T. D. McGlasson............................. Health Officer
Andrew Barry ....Engineer
Jas. M. Creighton......................................Architect
Henry Garfias ....Zanjero

PHŒNIX FIRE DEPARTMENT.

F. M. Czaruowski................................Chief Engineer
Frank D. Wells.......................Assistant Chief Engineer

PHŒNIX ENGINE CO. NO. 1.

W. J. Carrier ....Foreman
W. F. Schaller ....1st Assistant Foreman
T. L. Davenport ....2d Assistant Foreman
John Beck ....Secretary
E. J. Bennitt..Treasurer

PIONEER HOSE CO. NO. 1.

W. H. Levins..Foreman
A. E. Hinton ....1st Assistant Foreman
Wm. Black ....2d Assistant Foreman

YUCATEC HOSE CO. NO. 2.

C. Ceschetti..Foreman
Fernando Serrano.....................1st Assistant Foreman
W. Scott..............................2d Assistant Foreman

Aztec Hook and Ladder Co. No. 1.

J. L. Grant. . . . . Foreman
T. L. Schultz . . . . 1st Assistant Foreman
M. B. Fleishman . . . . 2d Assistant Foreman

FEDERAL AND COUNTY OFFICERS.

Hon. W. W. Porter. . . . . District Judge
J. Elliott Walker. . . . . Clerk
J. W. Crenshaw . . . . Court Commissioner
Frank Cox. . . . . District Attorney
—————————— . . . . Deputy U. S. Attorney
W. M. Breakenridge. . . . . Deputy U. S. Marshal
Joseph Campbell . . . . Probate Judge
A. J. Halbert . . . . Sheriff
Geo. F. Kemper. . . . . Treasurer
Henry L. Wharton. . . . . Recorder
Jno. B. Montgomery ⎫
H. H. Linville. . . . . ⎬ . . . . Supervisors
N. Petersen . . . . . . ⎭
J. L. B. Alexander . . . . Clerk Board of Supervisors
Jas. Richards. . . . . Justice of the Peace, Phœnix Precinct
W. T. Woods. . . . . Justice of the Peace, Phœnix Precinct
Wm. Blankenship. . . . . Constable, Phœnix Precinct
H. C. McDonald . . . . Constable, Phœnix Precinct

BOARD OF DIRECTORS TERRITORIAL INSANE ASYLUM.

E. H. Hiller . . . . Chairman
Emil Ganz . . . .
(Vacancy) . . . .
J. L. B. Alexander . . . . Clerk
Dr. O. L. Mahoney . . . . Superintendent

ARIZONA INDUSTRIAL EXPOSITION ASSOCIATION.

T. J. Trask . . . . President
Valley Bank . . . . Treasurer
J. McMillan. . . . . Secretary

DILLON & KENEALY, Leaders in Boots and Shoes.

MARICOPA COUNTY IMMIGRATION UNION.

T. J. Trask .... President
Valley Bank .... Treasurer
T. E. Farish .... Secretary

SECRET SOCIETIES.

MASONIC.

Arizona Chapter No. 1, R. A. M. Stated convocation on second Tuesday each month. F. A. Shaw, H. P.; J. B. Creamer, Secretary.

Arizona Lodge No. 2, F. & A. M. Stated meetings on first Tuesday each month. J. Y. T. Smith, W. M.; J. B. Creamer, Secretary.

Alsap Chapter No. 3, O. E. S. Stated meetings second and fourth Wednesdays each month. Mrs. A. M. Morford, W. M.; J. Y. T. Smith, Secretary

A. O. U. W.

Endymion Legion No. 5, A. O. U. W. Meets second and fourth Wednesday each month. Joseph Campbell, Commander, J. L. B. Alexander, Secretary.

Phœnix Lodge No. 5, A. O. U. W. Meets first and third Wednesday of each month. D. H. Recarte, M. W.; Joseph Campbell, Recorder.

I. O. O. F.

Canton Arizona No. 1, Patriarchs Militant, I. O. O. F. Meets third Tuesday evening each month. P. K. Hickey, Commandant; D. A. Reed, Clerk.

Floral Encampment No. 2, I. O. O. F. Meets second and fourth Tuesday evenings each month. P. K. Hickey, C. P.; D. A. Reed, Scribe.

Phœnix Lodge No. 2, I. O. O. F. Meets every Saturday evening. Robert Kern, N. G.; D. A. Reed, Secretary.

Arizona Degree Lodge No. 2, Daughters of Rebekah. Meets second and fourth Thursday evenings each month. Mrs. A. Schwartz, N. G.; C. S. Scott, Secretary.

I. O. G. T.

Garden Valley Lodge No. 1, I. O. G. T. Meets every Monday evening. T. L. Schultz, C. T., W. T. Woods, Jr., Secretary.

G. A. R.

John W. Owen Post No. 83, G. A. R. Meets in Masonic Hall on first Wednesday of every month. J. B. Creamer, P. C.; Allen T. Bird, Adj.

KNIGHTS OF PYTHIAS.

Phœnix Lodge No. 2. Meets on the first and third Fridays of each month in Pythian Hall. Webster Street, C. C.; J. A. Agard, K. of R.

O. C. F.

Phœnix Council No. 1. Meets first and third Thursdays of each month at Pythian Hall. Mrs. E. A. Ingalls, C. C.; Withrop Sears, Secretary.

U. O. OF H.

Cactus Lodge No. 137. Meets second and fourth Fridays of each mouth. J. E. Wharton, President; E. Irvine, Secretary.

PHŒNIX TYPOGRAPHICAL UNION, No. 237

Meets first Sunday in each month. Curt. W. Miller, President; J. E Bland, Secretary.

P. O. S. OF A.

Washington Camp No. 2. Meets every Thursday night in Masonic Hall. Robert Kern, President; L. H. Chalmers, Secretary.

PHŒNIX ✽ HOTEL,

BOB KERN, - - - *Proprietor.*

Enlarged and Improved.

New Furniture for the Year 1888

I shall pay special attention to the Dining Room, and all guests may depend on satisfactory attention, and a CUISINE that will embrace all delicacies obtainable.

NEATNESS,

PROMPTNESS,

ATTENTION.

Washington Street,

CLASSIFIED
BUSINESS DIRECTORY
CITY OF PHŒNIX.

Accountants
Hickey, P K
Reed, D A
Neustadter, I
Moore, Chas H

Amusements Places of
Patton Opera House
Garden City Theatre
Roller Skating Rink

Apothecaries (*see Druggists*)
Architects
Creighton, J M
McGinnis, W A
Petit, A P

Artists' Materials
Catton Brothers
Woods, W T, Jr

Attorneys at Law
Alexander, H N
Baker & Campbell
Chalmers, L H
Churchill, Clark
Cox, Frank I
Cox, Ivy H
Crenshaw, J W
Edwards, E J
Ford, J B   [rich
Goodrich, Smith, Street & Good-
Hancock, Wm A
Lemon & McCabe
Lighthizer, H B
Millay & Hine
Perley, Peleg S
Pinney, D H
Porter & Baxter
Wallace, D H

Auctioneers
Blankenship, J W
Mauk, G W

Bakeries
French Bakery
Phœnix Bakery
Vienna Bakery

Banks
Hartford Banking Co
National Bank of Arizona
Valley Bank, The

Barbers
Cota, Francisco
Lohman, E
Luhrs, J C H
McMurray, H E
Shumaker, H
Romero, Lazaro

Baths
Lohman, E
Shumaker, H
Swimming Bath

Bill Posters
Levins, Wm H
Mills, J H

Billiard Saloons
Commercial Hotel
Ceschetti & Bersanti
Luke & Johnson

Blacksmiths
Blake, W H
Burger, Jno H
Carrier, W J & Co

L. H. GOODRICH,
RESIDENT DENTIST,

OFFICE

Center Street, Opposite Goldman's, **PHŒNIX, ARIZONA.**

L. H. CHALMERS,
Attorney-at-Law,

Rooms 7 and 9, Thibodo Building, PHŒNIX, ARIZONA.

Pioneer Wine Vaults

—— AND ——

SAMPLE ROOMS.

The Only Reliable House at which to get Pure Wines and Liquors for Family and Medicinal Purposes.

PORTER BUILDING,

Center and Washington Sts., **PHŒNIX, ARIZONA.**

J. M. MONTANO, - - Proprietor.

OTIS ANDREWS & CO.,

Wholesale and Retail

FRUIT STORE

Packing and Shipping Salt River Valley Fruits and Produce A SPECIALTY.

GREEN GROCERIES, TOBACCO, FISH, GAME, ETC.

O. K. FRUIT STORE,

WASHINGTON STREET, Phœnix, Arizona.

2

Gardiner, J J & Co
Hulbert, W P
Nichols & Murray
McCarthy, James H
Orozco & Vasquez

Boarding Houses
Harriman, Mrs J
Knapp, Mrs C H
Philes, Mrs C E
Whitesides, Mrs R

Booksellers (*see News Depots*)

Bowling Alleys
Brix, Peter

Breweries
Arcade Brewery

Brick Manufacturers
Foushee, A S
Cox, M B
Marsh, J H A

Builders (*see Carpenters and Builders*)

Butchers
Amando, Manuel
Balsz & Co
Johnson, W M
Kelly & Marlow
Murray, D L & Co

Canal Companies
Arizona Canal Co
Buckeye Canal Co
Grand Canal Co
Highland Canal Co
Maricopa Canal Co
Salt River Valley Canal Co

Candy Manufacturers
Thomas, E W

Carriage and Wagon Makers
Moss, F B
McDonald, A
Nichols & Murray

Carriage and Wagon Repositories
Kemp, H E & Co
Goldman & Co

Carpenters and Builders
Bond & Hayden
Bury, C H
Byers, J S & Son
Creighton, J M
Gardiner, J J & Co
Harriman, J
Hershey, E S
Mills, C W
Patton, S E
Schriver, J M
Bridgeman, E E
Duhring, C
Collier, W C
Thomas, J H

Chinese Stores
See Yuen
Sam Wo Chung
Woh Lung & Co
Lem Quee
Hang Hong

Cigars and Tobacco
Hardy, Alex
Price, Geo
Seelig, T H

Civil Engineers
Barry, A
Breakenridge, Wm M
Davidson, S A
Hine, T W
Patrick, H R
Trott, F P

Clergymen
Cooper, E K (*Baptist*)
Fulton, S D (*Presbyterian*)
Jouvencean, F (*Catholic*)
McMullen, Thos H (*Christian*)
Norton, N F (*M E*)
Pearson, R W (*Episcopalian*)
Wright, C C (*M E South*)

Clothing(*see Dry Goods*)

Commission Merchants
Reynolds, J S

Commissioners of Deeds
Farish, T E

Contractors
Foushee, A S
Harmsen, B
Myers, L W
(*See also Carpenters and Builders*)

Copyists
Barbey, L E
Morris, C H
Neustadter, I

Dentists
Goodrich, L H
Happy Hour Dental Co
Small, K W

Draymen
Bewley, D S
Burnett, James K
Cable, W S
Coyle, P H
Green, Martin
McKean, F J

Dressmakers
Blythe, Mrs E A
Glassford, Miss M

Druggists
Eschman, C L & Co
Thibodo, O J

Dry Goods
Dillon & Kenealy
Ellis & Brown
Goldman & Co
Jacobs, M & Co
Winters, E H & Co

Employment Offices
Gallardo, Antonio G

Express
Wells, Fargo & Co

Fish Markets
Andrews & Hattox

Flour Mills
Smith, J Y T

Fruit Dealers '
Andrews, Otis & Co
Dorris, R B
Donofrio, C
Micca, G
Steinegger, Alex
Thomas, E W
(*See also Grocers*)

Furnishing Goods
Asher, A
Loring, Geo E
(*See also Dry Goods*)

Furniture
Schoenfeld & Heyman
Wohler, H & Co

Gas and Electric Light Co's
Phœnix Electric Light Co
Phœnix Illuminating Gas and
    Electric Light Co

Grocers
Farley & Grant
Goldberg, H
Goldman & Co
Jacobs, M & Co
Jeffries, L H
McNulty, W F
Sweeney & Recarte
Tauton & Kellner
Trask & Kays
Whepley, W L

Gunsmiths
Spangenberg, G F

Hackmen
Marshall, Alex

Hardware
Coon, Burtis & Coon
Goldman & Co
Kemp, Henry E & Co
Long, J B
Fowler, C D
Pesqueira, E

Harness and Saddlery
Andre, Robt G
Tulburt, H L

PHOENIX
ICE FACTORY.

S. D. LOUNT, Proprietor.

COR. PINAL & WASHINGTON STS.,

PHŒNIX, ARIZONA.

MARICOPA
Loan and Trust Company.

MONEY LOANED

On Real and Personal Security, long or short time,
as desired.

Correspondents and Eastern Agents: Northern Banking Co., Portland, Me.

JOSEPH W. SPAULDING, President,	-	Portland, Me.
JERRY MILLAY, General Manager,	-	Phœnix, Arizona.
MILFORD E. SPAULDING, Cashier,	-	Phœnix, Arizona.

Hatters
  Loring, Geo E
  (*See also Dry Goods*)

Horse Shoers (*see Blacksmiths*)

Hospitals
  Maricopa Co Hospital
  Terr Asylum for the Insane

Hotels and Lodging Houses
  Brown House
  Commercial Hotel
  Lemon Hotel
  Phœnix Hotel
  Gregory House
  Gilbert Lodging House
  Harriman Lodging House

Ice Factories
  Lount, S D & Son
  Minor, P

Insurance Agents
  Bennitt, E J
  Hickey Bros
  Fickas & Farish
  Finch, J H
  Kales, M W

Interpreters
  Barbey, L E (*French*)
  Holland, Jos (*Chinese*)
  Gallardo, A G (*Spanish*)
  Righetti, J P (*Italian*)   [copa
  Morgan, Henry (*Pima and Mari-*

Japanese Bazaars
  Lem Que
  Hang Hong

Jewelers
  Curry, W J
  Humphrey, R J
  Joyeau, Victor
  Nilson, P F

Laundries
  Phœnix Steam Laundry

Laundries Chinese
  Wing Lee
  Wan Sing
  Quong Lee

  Gee Hop
  Sing Lee
  Sam Wing
  Chung Hing
  Fang Sang
  Wing Hi
  Quong Woh

Lawyers (*see Attorneys at Law*)

Libraries
  Phœnix Library Association
  W C T U Library

Liquor Dealers, Wholesale
  Goldman & Co
  R Ruben, Son & Co
  Ganz, E
  Montano, J M

Liquor Dealers, Retail
  Barnard, Geo W
  Brix, Peter
  Ceschetti & Bersanti
  Daneri, Estefano
  Ganz, E
  Jensen, J H W
  Kern, Robt
  Loosley, J R
  Luke & Johnson
  Luke, John
  Montano, J M
  McNamara J M
  Martini, J
  Pimm & Butler
  Pawley, James
  Righetti, James
  Sanders, M M
  Short, O A
  Thalheimer, J

Livery Stables
  Herrick & Luhrs
  Fuqua, Frank
  Grant, J L
  Gibson, J M
  McCann, W S
  Ward, J L & Sons

Locksmiths
  Byers, J S
  Spangenberg, G F

DILLON & KENEALY, Leaders in Hats.

PHŒNIX BAKERY,
Confectionery and Ice Cream

PARLORS,

MANUFACTURERS OF

Candies and all kinds of Confectionery.

CARRY A FULL LINE OF

NUTS, FRESH FRUITS, BREAD, ROLLS, BUNS,
*All kinds of Pies, which are baked and
delivered free, daily, to all
parts of the City.*

WE ALSO CARRY THE

Choicest Brands of Cigars, Smoking & Chewing Tobacco.

PORTER BUILDING, PHŒNIX, ARIZONA.

LEWIS & HERLICK,   -   -   Proprietors.

E. PESQUEIRA,

DEALER IN

STOVES, TINWARE, GRANITE

And Agate Ironware, Etc., Etc.

*Roofing and Gas Fitting receives our special and careful attention.
Driven Wells a Specialty.*

East Side of Capital Plaza, - Phœnix, Arizona.

E. H. THOMAS,

CANDY MANUFACTURER, CONFECTIONER,

AND DEALER IN

FRESH FRUITS, NUTS, CIGARS AND TOBACCO.

ICE CREAM, SODA WATER & FRESH OYSTERS

IN THEIR SEASON.

Washington Street, opposite City Hall,

PHŒNIX, ARIZONA.

Lumber Yards
Blinn, L W & Co
Gregory, J M
Ryder, H W

Lunch Counters
Butler, Ben
Schlessinger, S V

Meat Markets (see Butchers)

Miscellaneous Corporations
(Not otherwise classified)
Arizona Improvement Co
Phœnix Street Railway Co
Phœnix City Water Works Co
Maricopa Co Immigration Union
Maricopa Loan & Trust Co
Arizona Indust'l Exposit'n Assc'n
Maricopa Brownstone Quarry Co
Maricopa Vineyard Co
Valley Abstract Co

Milk Dealers
Hurley, C C
Kellogg, Wm
Montgomery, J B

Milliners
Blythe, Mrs E A
Curtis, Mrs N J

Mineral Water
Josselyn & Smyley

Mining Companies
Phœnix Mining Co
Union Mining Co   [M & M Co
Trinidad and Castle Creek
Clarence Ruby Gold M & M Co

Music Teachers
Shook, Prof L B
Schulenburg, Prof Ad

News Depots   .
Catton Bros
Woods, W T, Jr

Newspapers
Arizona Gazette (daily & weekly)
Arizonan, The (daily & weekly)
Phœnix Herald (daily & weekly)
Phœnix Weekly Advance

Notaries Public
Baxter, Frank
Cox, Frank
Chalmers, L H
Fickas, B A
Fowler, L
Franklin, A M
Fulwiler, W D
Gallardo, A G
Hickey, Jno J
Hoadley, Geo W
Hickey, P K
Hirschfeld, G H
Hancock, Wm A
Ingalls, G W
Martin, Geo T
Perley, P S
Reed, D A
Utley, A A
Walker, J W
Wallace, D H

Nurseries
Garden City Nursery,
          Devereux, F B, prop
Phœnix Nursery,
          Farrington, R E, prop
Paradise Nursery, Turner, D, prop
Collier's Nursery, Collier, W C, agt

Oyster Saloons
Thomas, E W
Steinegger, A

Painters
Fritz, the Painter
Rixen, Henry
Sears, Winthrop
White, Jno Q

Photographers
Catton, C W
Rothrock, G H

Physicians
Pourquie, L
Hong Kong, (Chinese)
Hughes & McGlasson
Ingalls, Mrs E A
Lightburne, R E
McDougall, E
Osborne, R T
Rosson, R L

L. W. BLINN
Lumber Company.

PHŒNIX BRANCH.

L. W. BLINN, General Manager, - - Tombstone, Arizona.
SAN FRANCISCO OFFICE, - - - 4 California Street.

✦LUMBER✦

Fancy and Plain Doors,
Sash, Blinds,
Lime, Hair,
Cement, Plaster,
Laths,
Wood Ornaments,
And Cut and Embossed Fancy Glass.

BUILDERS' HARDWARE.

OFFICE,
Cor. Montezuma and Adams Sts.

Yards, on Tonto St.,
NEAR M. & P. R. R. DEPOT.

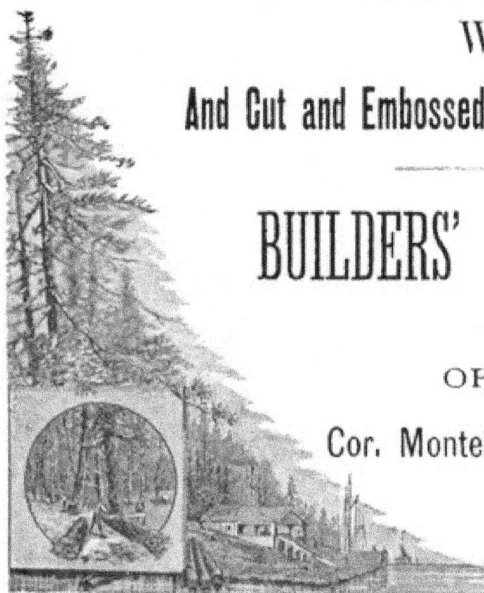

Stern, L
Thibodo, O J
Wharton, J E
Mahoney, O L
Mahoney, Mrs Virginia

Piano Dealers
Redeuil, A
Shook, L B

Planing Mills
Gardiner, J J & Co

Plasterers
Atkinson, J P
Harmsen, B
Evans, Henry

Printing Offices (see Newspapers)

Produce and Vegetables
(See Grocers.)

Railroads
Maricopa & Phœnix R R
Phœnix Street Railway Co

R. R. Ticket Brokers
Goldberg, Aaron
Price, George
Seelig, T H

Real Estate Dealers
Arizona Land & Reclamation Co
Bird, Allen T
Collins, M E
Evans, J W
Fowler Bros
Franklin & Thomas
Hickey Bros
Hancock, Wm A
Holmes & Hewins
Irvine, E
Jackman, S H
Johnstone, C W
Logan & Allen
Perkins & Walker
Phœnix Land Investment Co
Porter & Baxter
Real Estate & Mining Exchange
Symonds & Bird
Wallace, D H
Schultz & Franklin

Restaurants
Boss Restaurant
Cabinet Restaurant
Garden City Restaurant
Grand Central Restaurant
Chung Ty Restaurant
Star Restaurant
French Restaurant
Capitol Restaurant

Second-hand Store
Dorris Bros

Sewing Machine Agencies
Dillard, P F
Lewis, Q A

Shoemakers
Moreno, A
Pfeiffer, Geo A
Sanchez, A

Stables (see Livery Stables)

Stage Lines
Arizona Stage Co
Tempe & McDowell Stage Line

Stationers (see News Depots)

Steamship Agencies
Meyer, A Leonard

Stenographers
Pinney, W L
Rosenberg, G A

Stoves and Tinware (see Hardware)

Surveyors (see Civil Engineers)

Tailors
Eisenbardt, F
Landgraf, Geo
Martinez, Victoriano
Merchant Tailor Agency,
      H S Bridge & Co

Teachers—Public and Private Schools
Baker, Miss M
Bury, Mrs C H
Davis, Mrs W A
Dalton, Prof T A
Dole, Miss Julia

Fulton, Mrs A A
Fry, Miss Lillian
Kelly, Miss Ada
Kelly, Miss Addie
Lynch, Miss M
McDermott, Miss Letitia
Sweeney, Mrs J J
Warren, Miss Edna V

Telegraph Companies
U S Military Tel
Arizona Telegraph Co

Tobacconists (*see Cigars and Tobacco*)

Undertakers
Bacon, J A
Gregory, J M
Ryder, H W
Wohler, H & Co

Veterinary Surgeons
Chandler, A J
Keefer, Geo H

Watchmakers (*see Jewelers*)

SOUTHERN PACIFIC CO.

(PACIFIC SYSTEM.)

TICKET RATES BETWEEN MARICOPA

AND STATIONS NAMED BELOW.

Children under twelve years of age, half **Fare.** *Children under five years of age, free.*

To obtain Rates from Phœnix, add $3.00 to Rates from Maricopa.

Stations.	Unlimited 1st Class.	2d Class.	Stations.	Unlimited 1st Class.	2d Class
San Francisco	33 85	25 00	Avon	33 60	25 00
Oakland, 16th St	33 85	25 00	Cornwall	33 30	25 00
West Berkeley	33 85	25 00	Los Medanos	33 20	25 00
Stege	33 85	25 00	Antioch	33 15	25 00
San Pablo	33 85	25 00	Brentwood	32 90	25 00
Sobrante	33 85	25 00	Byron	32 75	25 00
Pinole	33 85	25 00	Bethany	32 45	25 00
Vallejo Junction	33 85	25 00	Tracy	32 25	25 00
Port Costa	33 85	25 00	Banta	32 15	25 00
Martinez	33 70	25 00	Lathrop	31 85	25 00

DILLON & KENEALY, One Price Square Dealers.

FRANK COX,

ATTORNEY-AT-LAW,

Special attention given to collections.   District Attorney for Maricopa County.

A. C. BAKER.   JOE CAMPBELL.

BAKER & CAMPBELL,

ATTORNEYS-AT-LAW,

Rooms 1 and 2, Thibodo Building,   Phœnix, Arizona.

PHŒNIX

STEAM FLOUR MILLS

AND FAMILY GROCERY STORE,

Cor. Montezuma and Jefferson Sts., - Phœnix, Arizona.

JOHN Y. T. SMITH, Proprietor.

P. O. Box 78.

H. L. TULBURT,

DEALER IN AND MANUFACTURER OF

SADDLES, HARNESS,

—— AND ——

Horse Furnishing Goods of all Descriptions.

CARRIAGE TRIMMING AND REPAIRING

NEATLY DONE AND SATISFACTION GUARANTEED.

SHOP, WASHINGTON STREET, NEAR HARTFORD BANK,

PHOENIX, ARIZONA.

Have served apprenticeship in all lines of my business and have worked in over twenty States and Territories. I am thoroughly posted in all styles of Stock Saddles and Light and Heavy Harness. All my work is hand-made, and

THE BEST OF LEATHER USED.

Stations.	Unlimited 1st Class.		2d Class.	Stations.	Unlimited 1st Class.		2d Class.
Ripon	31	55	25 00	Saugus	19	80	
Salida	31	45	25 00	Fillmore	20	50	
Modesto	31	25	25 00	Santa Paula	20	80	
Ceres	31	15	25 00	Saticoy	21	05	
Turlock	30	85	25 00	Conejo	21	15	
Delhi	30	70	25 00	San Buenaventura	21	30	
Livingston	30	55	25 00	Carpinteria	21	85	
Atwater	30	35	25 00	Monticeto	22	05	
Merced	30	15	25 00	Santa Barbara	22	15	
Athlone	29	85	25 00	Saugus	19	80	
Minturn	29	65	25 00	Newhall	19	75	
Berenda	29	35	25 00	Fernando	19	45	
Raymond	31	35	27 00	Burbank	19	15	
Berenda	29	35	25 00	Sepulveda	19	10	
Madera	29	15	25 00	Tropico	19	00	
Borden	29	05	25 00	Los Angeles	18	85	
Sycamore	28	80	25 00	Ballona	19	15	
Fresno	28	50	25 00	The Palms	19	20	
Malaga	28	35	25 00	Santa Monica	19	35	
Fowler	28	20	25 00	Los Angeles	18	85	
Selma	28	05	25 00	Florence	19	00	
Kingsburg	27	90	25 00	Lynwood	19	15	
Traver	27	70	25 00	Compton	19	15	
Goshen	27	50	25 00	Cerritos	19	30	
Hanford	27	85	25 40	Wilmington	19	35	
Lemoore	28	10	25 65	San Pedro	19	45	
Huron	28	75	26 25	Los Angeles	18	85	
Goshen	27	50	25 00	Florence	19	00	
Tulare	27	15	25 00	Downey	19	20	
Tokay	27	00	25 00	Norwalk	19	35	
Tipton	26	85	25 00	Anaheim	19	65	
Pixley	26	65	25 00	Orange	19	80	
Alila	26	50	25 00	Santa Ana	19	85	
Delano	26	25	25 00	Los Angeles	18	85	
Sumner	25	25	25 00	Shorb	18	65	
Pampa	24	65		Alhambra	18	60	
Caliente	24	35		San Gabriel	18	55	
Keene	23	80		Savanna	18	50	
Girard	23	60		Monte	18	45	
Tehachapi	23	35		Puente	18	25	
Cameron	23	00		Spadra	17	95	
Mojave	22	55		Pomona	17	85	
Lancaster	21	55		Ontario	17	65	
Alpine	21	10		Cucamonga	17	55	
Southside	20	55		Colton	17	10	
Lang	20	25		Mound City	17	00	
Kent	20	15		Brookside	16	90	

Stations.	Unlimited 1st Class.	2d Class.	Stations.	Unlimited 1st Class.	2d Class.
El Casco	16 65		San Francisco	33 85	25 00
San Gorgonio	16 40		Oakland, Market St.	33 85	25 00
Banning	16 20		East Oakland	33 85	25 00
Indio	14 05		Fruit Vale	33 85	25 00
Yuma	8 10		Melrose	33 85	25 00
Gila City	7 40		San Leandro	33 85	25 00
Adonde	6 60		Lorenzo	33 85	25 00
Tacna	6 10		Haywards	33 85	25 00
Mohawk Summit	5 30		Decoto	33 75	25 00
Texas Hill	4 95		Niles	33 65	25 00
Aztec	4 30		Irvington	33 75	25 00
Stanwix	3 85		Warm Springs	33 85	25 00
Sentinel	3 60		Milpitas	33 85	25 00
Painted Rock	2 90		San Jose	33 85	25 00
Gila Bend	2 15		Niles	33 65	25 00
Bosque	1 65		Sunol	33 45	25 00
Estrella	1 20		Pleasanton	33 30	25 00
Montezuma	75		Livermore	33 10	25 00
Heaton	25		Altamont	32 80	25 00
Sweet Water	50		Midway	32 55	25 00
Casa Grande	1 05		Tracy	32 25	25 00
Toltec	1 55		Lathrop	31 85	25 00
Picacho	2 00		Stockton	32 20	25 00
Red Rock	2 70		Charleston	32 45	25 25
Sandair	3 20		Milton	33 40	26 20
Rillito	3 50		Peters	32 80	25 60
Jaynes	4 00		Farmington	33 00	25 80
Tucson	4 35		Oakdale	33 55	26 35
Wilmot	4 65		Stockton	32 20	25 00
Papago	5 05		Lodi	32 65	25 00
Pantano	5 75		Galt	32 90	25 00
Mescal	6 20		Carbondale	33 75	25 85
Benson	6 65		Ione	34 00	26 10
Ochoa	7 10		Galt	32 90	25 00
Dragoon Summit	7 60		Elk Grove	33 30	25 00
Cachise	8 10		Florin	33 55	25 00
Willcox	8 65		Brighton	33 65	25 00
Bowie	9 80		Sacramento	33 85	25 00
San Simon	10 60		Antelope	34 30	25 45
Steins Pass	11 35		Junction	34 40	25 55
Lordsburg	12 30		Lincoln	34 75	25 90
Lisbon	12 85		Sheridan	34 95	26 10
Separ	13 30		Wheatland	35 05	26 20
Deming	15 30		Yuba	35 40	26 55
El Paso	19 65		Marysville	35 45	26 60
			Gridley	35 95	27 10
			Biggs	36 05	27 20

Stations.	Unlimited 1st Class.	2d Class.	Stations.	Unlimited 1st Class.	2d Class.
Nelson	36 35	27 50	Reno	40 90	32 05
Durham	36 55	27 70	Wadsworth	42 60	33 75
Chico	36 75	27 90	Oreana	46 30	37 45
Nord	36 95	28 10	Humboldt	47 40	38 55
Vina	37 00	28 35	Winnemucca	49 40	40 55
Tehama	37 00	28 35	Golconda	50 20	41 35
Red Bluff	37 35	28 70	Battle Mountain	52 40	43 55
Cottonwood	37 85	29 20	Beowawe	54 05	45 20
Anderson	38 05	29 40	Palisade	54 95	46 10
Redding	38 40	29 75	Carlin	55 40	46 55
Middle Creek	38 55	29 90	Moleen	56 00	47 10
Kennet	39 10	30 45	Elko	56 55	47 10
Elmore	39 45	30 80	Halleck	57 75	47 10
Smithson	39 75	31 10	Wells	59 40	47 10
Delta	39 95	31 30	Independence	60 15	47 10
Gibson	40 25	31 60	Toano	61 20	47 10
Castle Creek	40 70	32 05	Montello	62 00	47 10
Lower Soda Springs	40 80	32 15	Tecoma	62 50	47 10
Dunsmuir	41 00	32 35	Terrace	64 15	47 10
Upper Soda Springs	41 00	32 35	Kelton	65 75	47 10
McCloud	41 45	32 80	Promontory	66 85	47 10
Sisson	41 55	32 90	Corinne	66 85	47 10
Edgewood	42 25	33 60	Brigham	66 85	47 10
Montague	43 10	34 45	Bonneville	66 85	47 10
Snowdon	43 35	34 70	*Ogden*	66 85	47 10
Hornbrook	43 80	35 15	*South Vallejo*	34 00	25 15
Coles	44 15	35 50	*Napa Junction*	34 25	25 40
Junction	34 40	25 55	Cordelia	34 45	25 60
Rocklin	34 55	25 70	*Napa Junction*	34 25	25 40
Penryn	34 70	25 85	Napa	34 50	25 65
Newcastle	34 80	25 95	Yountville	34 75	25 90
Auburn	34 95	26 10	Oakville	34 85	26 00
Clipper Gap	35 30	26 45	Rutherford	34 90	26 05
Lander	35 75	26 90	St. Helena	35 05	26 20
Colfax	35 90	27 05	*Calistoga*	35 30	26 45
Cape Horn Mills	36 10	27 25	*Port Costa*	33 85	25 00
Gold Run	36 40	27 55	*Benicia*	33 95	25 10
Dutch Flat	36 50	27 65			
Shady Run	36 85	28 00			
Blue Cañon	37 10	28 25			
Emigrant Gap	37 35	28 50			
Cisco	37 75	28 90			
Tamarack	37 95	29 10			
Cascade	38 15	29 30			
Summit	38 45	29 60			
Truckee	39 15	30 30			
Boca	39 55	30 70			

SOUTHERN PACIFIC COMPANY.

THROUGH RATES OF FARE.

(SUBJECT TO CHANGE.)

To obtain rates from Phœnix, add $3.00 to rates from Maricopa.

From Maricopa.	Unlimited. 1st Class.	Limited. 2d Class.	From Maricopa.	Unlimited. 1st Class.	Limited. 2d Class.
Baltimore, Md	$81 45	$59 00	Milwaukee, Wis	$65 00	$48 50
Binghampton, N. Y.	79 90	60 00	Montreal, Can	84 35	62 50
Birmingham, Ala	63 20	46 70	Nashville, Tenn	61 75	46 70
Boston, Mass	85 85	63 50	New Orleans, La	57 10	42 50
Buffalo, N. Y.	75 20	56 95	New York, N. Y.	84 45	61 50
Burlington, Ia	61 85		Omaha, Neb	59 70	39 75
Cairo, Ill	57 20	42 50	Pacific Junction, Ia.	59 70	39 75
Chattanooga, Tenn.	64 30	49 00	Philadelphia, Pa	84 15	60 00
Chicago, Ill	66 05		Pittsburg, Pa	74 75	55 50
Cincinnati, Ohio	69 80	50 50	Portland, Me	89 35	66 50
Cleveland, Ohio	72 30	54 45	Quebec, Can	86 20	63 85
Columbus, Ohio	71 30	52 65	Quincy, Ill	59 70	
Council Bluffs, Ia.	59 65	39 75	Richmond, Va	86 50	61 60
Dayton, Ohio	70 30	50 50	Rochester, N. Y.	76 60	58 30
Denver, Col	45 65	30 00	Rock Island, Ill	62 95	
Detroit, Mich	73 80	53 35	Salamanca, N. Y.	76 15	56 90
Erie, Pa	73 50	55 85	Sandusky, Ohio	73 30	53 00
Evansville, Ind	64 80	46 70	Springfield, Ill	61 45	46 95
Fitchburg, Mass.	89 60	63 75	Springfield, Mass	84 15	62 50
Fort Wayne, Ind	69 50	50 50	Springfield, Ohio	71 30	51 20
Fort Worth, Tex	38 10	35 00	St. Louis, Mo	59 45	
Galveston, Tex	46 00	35 90	St. Joseph, Mo	55 75	37 05
Harrisburg, Pa	82 20	59 00	St. Paul, Minn	69 95	45 00
Houston, Tex	45 15	35 00	Syracuse, N. Y.	78 20	59 90
Indianapolis, Ind	65 15		Toledo, Ohio	71 30	52 20
Kansas City, Mo.	54 90	35 00	Washington, D. C.	81 45	59 00
London, Can	72 60	56 75	Wheeling, W. Va	73 00	55 75
Louisville, Ky	66 00	49 25	Youngstown, Ohio	75 20	56 25
Memphis, Tenn	54 75	42 50	Zanesville, Ohio	71 85	53 40

Above rates apply via direct routes only.

Ask agents for rates to other and intermediate destinations.

Children under twelve (12) years of age, half fare.

Children under five (5) years of age, free.

150 lbs. free baggage will be allowed per each whole ticket.

WELLS, FARGO & CO.

EXPRESS AND BANKING.

Capital, - - - - - $6,250,000.

JNO. J. VALENTINE................ General Manager, San Francisco
E. M. COOPER....General Sup't, Western Department, San Francisco
L. F. ROWELL .... Sup't, Southwestern Division, San Francisco

A. LEONARD MEYER, Agent, Phœnix, Arizona.

(Over 1,900 Agencies throughout the United States and Mexico.)

The business of Wells, Fargo & Co's Express, is to forward, by rapid conveyance,

**Merchandise, Packages,
Parcels, Jewelry,
Gold, Silver,
Bank Notes, Bonds,
Valuable Papers, Etc.,**

and to deliver the same promptly ; to make collections, with or without goods ; to fill orders, attend to commissions and to carry and deliver letters.

The Company's lines extend throughout the Western States, from the

PACIFIC OCEAN TO CHICAGO, ST. LOUIS AND NEW ORLEANS,

where connections are made with responsible Express Companies for other points in the United States and Canada, throughout the Republic of Mexico, to Asiatic ports and to nearly all the principal Cities of Europe.

WHO IS
H. SHUMAKER ?

Replying to the Question you just asked,
we will quote from a local Newspaper.

"He has without doubt the neatest Barber Shop in this country; it is supplied with six Monarch Chairs, made by E. Berminghaus, Cincinnati, Ohio. For beauty and comfort these chairs stand without an equal. Grand in construction, stately in appearance, ornamental in design, fine in finish, the leading chair of the nineteenth century. The mirror case standing in front of these chairs is thirty feet long; all the woodwork is black walnut, carved, veneered and engraved. The shelf is of pure Italian marble. The whole is fitted with French plate mirrors, 50 by 60 inches. A large plate glass mirror is placed over the wash stand and a magnificent dressing case ornaments one side of the room.

"The wash stand and bathrooms are supplied with hot and cold clear water. The barber shop and bathrooms are illuminated by gas, giving the whole place a brilliant appearance, and, as we said before, making without exception, the finest and most complete barber shop and bathrooms in this country. Six men who thoroughly understand their business are continually employed to attend to the wants of patrons. Mr. Shumaker is too well known among our people to need any further mention; he is an old-time barber and an old Arizonian. Phœnix ought to be proud that she possesses a man of his stability and enterprise."

ISAAC OROZCO.   ADOLFO VASQUEZ.

BLACKSMITHS AND FARRIERS.

Wagon-making and Repairing a Specialty.

All Kinds of Wagon and Iron Work Skillfully Executed.

OROZCO & VASQUEZ,

Cor. Cortez & Madison Sts.,   -   PHŒNIX, ARIZONA.

PURCHASING
—AND—
COMMISSION DEPARTMENT.

TRADING, ETC., BY EXPRESS.

The object of this Department is to give the public the use of the vast facilities controlled by and within the reach of

Wells, Fargo & Co's Express,

for satisfying their most peculiar wants in the well-furnished markets of cities and towns.

A Trial will convince any Person of its Great Advantages

over the old-fashioned and inconsiderate practice of *imposing upon friends and acquaintances*, when traveling, all sorts of troublesome and unprofitable commissions, or *intrusting them to unknown and irresponsible parties*.

No Invasion of Local Mercantile Interests

is made or contemplated by it; for it is more particularly designed to meet those cases of frequent occurrence when a particular article is wanted—*something that cannot possibly be had in the home market*. The truth of this assertion will not be disputed if the expense of service and express charges, added to cost of purchase, are taken into account. In its legitimate province, the PURCHASING AND COMMISSION DEPARTMENT of this Company is *not hurtful to any business interest*, and those who have tried it—*business firms and private families*—understand well that it is

A GREAT PUBLIC CONVENIENCE,

and find many occasions to resort to it. Through their agents in every city, village or railway station of any importance, and the thousands of employees, scattered up and down the country within their own jurisdiction, and their correspondents and

Business Connections in Large Cities, at Home and Abroad,

and with other Express Companies, they certainly have the appliances at command for operating this peculiar branch of business in the most thorough and satisfactory manner.

VARIETY STOCK FARM,

6 Miles West of Phœnix, on the Yuma Road.

+FORREST CLAY+

Register, No. 1934.

Forrest Clay, the celebrated Kentucky trotting horse, the only standard bred Stallion in the Territory, will make the season, beginning MARCH 1st and ending JUNE 1st, 1888, in PHŒNIX the first four days of each week, and at VARIETY STOCK FARM the last three days of each week.

TERMS—$50.00 to insure. Secured note taken, payable at end of the season.

A few standard bred stallion colts, from Forrest Clay, out of imported mares from Gen. W. T. Withers' Fairlawn Stock Farm, Lexington, Ky., for sale.

All mares being bred to Forrest Clay will be given pasture free during season.

BLUE GRASS BOY.

No. 65,285.

The thoroughbred Durham Bull, from the Abe Renick's Rose of Sharon tribe, is at the Variety Stock Farm. Service $10.00 per cow, a calf guaranteed. Thoroughbred and graded bull calves for sale from this noted bull, which was purchased from W. W. Hamilton, of Lexington, Ky., and imported by Geo. T. Beckers.

THOROUGHBRED

Registered Berkshire and Poland

CHINA HOGS.

Having purchased the entire band of thoroughbred Berkshire and Poland China Hogs, imported by G. W. F. Johnson, for the Calistoga Stock Farm, I will sell pigs in lots of three (one boar and two sows) for $25.00. The pedigree of all thoroughbred stock guaranteed. For further particulars inquire of or address,

GEO. T. BECKERS, Phœnix, A. T.

PURCHASING ᴬᴺᴰ COMMISSION DEPARTMENT.

TELEGRAPHIC ORDERS.

Special telegraphic orders through the Company's agents will always receive prompt attention, the cost of telegram being prepaid by the party for whom it is sent.

BAGGAGE CHECKS

May be sent to this Department.   Care should be taken to keep a memorandum of the numbers. They should be regularly way-billed, with charges *prepaid*.

PAWNBROKERS' TICKETS

Sent to redeem property, must be accompanied by the full amount due.   Pawnbrokers as a rule, will not forward pledges C. O. D.

SPECIAL COMMISSIONS.

In connection with the Purchasing and Commission Department, proper attention will be given to the *Recording of Deeds*, and the *Service of Legal Papers* in any county where the Company have an agency, and to *business connected with the various Departments at State and Territorial Capitals.*   The public should bear this fact in mind.

The Purchasing and Commission Department

is under the supervision of Mr. Aaron Stein, an experienced and conscientious gentleman, well and favorably known to the business community of San Francisco, and to the Express fraternity throughout the entire country, who will spare no pains to give prompt and entire satisfaction.   All orders will be filled and returned as soon as possible.

Express rates, per 100 lbs., from Phœnix to ALL offices in

ARIZONA.

Ash Fork	$11 25	Alviso	$ 8 00
Bellemont	11 50	Amador	10 50
Benson	4 25	Anaheim	7 50
Bowie	5 50	Antioch	7 50
Calabasas	5 25	Arcata	10 25
Cañon Diablo	12 25	Arroyo Grande	13 25
Casa Grande	1 75	Auburn	8 50
Clifton	8 75	Bakersfield	7 50
Contention	4 75	Banning	7 00
Crittenden	5 00	Barstow	8 50
Dragoon	4 50	Benicia	8 10
Duncan	7 75	Berenda	7 50
Fairbank	4 75	Berkeley	7 50
Flagstaff	11 75	Bishop Creek	15 00
Florence	5 25	Bloomfield	9 00
Gila Bend	2 25	Blue Cañon	9 50
Globe	12 75	Bodega	9 10
Hackberry	10 75	Bodie	17 00
Holbrook	12 25	Borden	7 50
Huachuca	4 75	Butte City	10 25
Kingman	10 50	Caliente	7 50
Maricopa	1 00	Calistoga	8 50
Navajo Springs	12 25	Cambria	14 75
Nogales	5 25	Camp Taylor	8 25
Pantano	3 75	Castroville	8 25
Peach Springs	10 75	Carlsbad	8 25
Pinal	8 50	Cloverdale	8 50
Prescott	17 75	Colfax	9 00
Prescott Junction	11 25	Colton	7 00
San Simon	6 00	Colusa	9 10
Sentinel	3 00	Concord	8 50
Tempe	0 50	Copperopolis	9 75
Texas Hill	3 50	Cordelia	8 25
Tombstone	6 25	Crescent City	10 50
Tucson	3 25	Cucamonga	7 00
Willcox	5 00	Daggett	8 50
Williams	11 50	Davisville	8 10
Winslow	12 25	Delano	7 50
Yucca	10 25	Delta	10 00
Yuma	4 75	Diamond Springs	9 50
		Dixon	8 25
		Downey	7 50
		Downieville	15 50
		Duncan Mills	8 90
		Dutch Flat	9 25

Express rates, per 100 lbs., from Phœnix to following offices in

CALIFORNIA.

		East Oakland	7 50
		Elmira	8 25
		Elsinore	8 00
		Emigrant Gap	9 50
Alameda	$8 00	Encinitas	8 25
Alma	8 00	Eureka	9 75
Alturas	21 00	Farmington	8 00
Alvarado	8 00	Felton	8 50

Ferndale	$11	75	Los Alamos	$13	75
Firebaughs	11	00	Los Angeles	7	00
Folsom	8	00	Los Banos	12	25
Fort Jones	14	00	Los Gatos	8	00
Fowler	7	50	Lower Lake	12	00
Freestone	8	75	Madera	7	50
French Gulch	11	50	Madison	8	75
Fresno	7	50	Mariposa	12	50
Fulton	8	25	Martinez	7	50
Galt	7	50	Marysville	8	25
Gilroy	8	00	Mayfield	8	00
Glen Ellen	8	40	Mendocino	15	00
Glenwood	8	25	Menlo Park	8	00
Gold Run	9	25	Merced	7	50
Goshen	7	50	Michigan Bar	9	50
Grass Valley	9	50	Millbrae	8	00
Grayson	9	25	Millville	11	00
Gridley	8	50	Milpitas	7	50
Gualala	12	50	Milton	8	00
Guerneville	8	50	Modesto	7	50
Hanford	7	50	Mojave	7	50
Haywards	7	50	Monterey	8	50
Healdsburg	8	50	Mountain View	8	00
Highland Springs	10	90	Napa	8	10
Hildreth	9	75	National City	8	25
Hill's Ferry	9	25	Needles	9	75
Hollister	8	25	Nevada	9	50
Howards	8	90	Newark	8	00
Hueneme	10	00	Newcastle	8	50
Huron	7	50	Newhall	7	50
Independence	16	00	Niles	7	50
Ione	8	00	Nord	9	00
Iowa Hill	10	75	Norwalk	7	50
Irvington	7	50	Oakdale	8	00
Jackson	10	50	Oakland	7	50
Jamestown	12	25	Oceanside	8	25
Keeler	16	00	Olema	8	50
Kelseyville	11	25	Ontario	7	00
Kernville	12	50	Orange	7	50
Kingsburg	7	50	Oroville	8	75
Knight's Landing	8	40	Pasadena	7	50
Knoxville	11	50	Paso Robles	9	25
Lakeport	11	25	Pescadero	11	25
Lamanda	7	50	Petaluma	8	00
Lancaster	7	50	Placerville	9	50
La Porte	14	50	Pleasanton	7	50
Lathrop	7	50	Plymouth	10	50
Lemoore	7	50	Point Arenas	13	50
Lincoln	8	25	Pomona	7	00
Livermore	7	50	Port Costa	7	50
Lodi	7	50	Portersville	9	50
Lompoc	15	75	Quincy	14	75
Lone Pine	16	00	Raymond	8	00

Red Bluff	$9 40	Susanville	$14 50
Redding	9 50	Sutter Creek	10 50
Redwood City	8 00	Sweetland	11 50
Rio Vista	8 25	Tahoe	11 50
Riverside	7 25	Tchachapi	7 50
Rocklin	8 25	Tehama	9 25
Rohnerville	11 75	Temecula	7 75
Sacramento	7 50	Templeton	9 25
St. Helena	8 50	Tipton	7 50
Salinas	8 50	Tomales	8 50
San Andreas	10 00	Tres Pinos	8 50
San Anselmo	8 10	Truckee	10 25
San Ardo	9 00	Tulare	7 50
San Bernardino	7 25	Ukiah	12 00
San Buenaventura	9 00	Upper Lake	11 75
San Diego	8 25	Vacaville	8 75
San Fernando	7 50	Vallejo	8 00
San Francisco	7 50	Vina	9 10
San Gabriel	7 00	Visalia	8 00
San Gorgonio	11 00	Watsonville	8 25
San Jose	7 50	Weaverville	13 50
San Juan	9 25	West Berkeley	7 50
San Leandro	7 50	West Oakland	7 50
San Luis Obispo	12 75	Westport	16 50
San Mateo	8 00	Wheatland	8 25
San Miguel	9 00	Williams	8 75
San Pablo	7 50	Willows	8 75
San Pedro	7 50	Wilmington	7 50
San Quentin	8 00	Windsor	8 25
San Rafael	8 00	Winters	8 75
Santa Ana	7 50	Woodland	8 25
Santa Barbara	9 50	Yolo	8 50
Santa Clara	8 00	Yosemite	16 00
Santa Cruz	8 25	Yountville	8 25
Santa Maria	13 50	Yreka	12 50
Santa Monica	7 50		
Santa Paula	8 50		
Santa Rosa	8 25		
Saucelito	8 00		

Express rates, per 100 lbs., from Phœnix to following offices in

COLORADO.

Denver	$13 50
Fort Morgan	14 80
Las Animas	13 00
La Junta	13 00
Longmont	14 25
Pueblo	12 50
Trinidad	12 50

Selma	7 50
Shasta	10 25
Sierra City	17 00
Smartsville	10 00
Soledad	8 75
Sonoma	8 25
Sonora	12 25
Soquel	8 25
Spadia	7 00
Spanishtown	10 00
Stockton	7 50
Strawberry Valley	12 75
Suisun	8 10
Sumner	7 50

Express rates, per 100 lbs., from Phœnix to following offices in

DAKOTA.

Bismarck	$23 50
Colfax	19 90

Commercial
HOTEL,

HERRICK & LUHRS, Proprietors.

THE

Leading Business and Family Hotel

IN ARIZONA.

Containing 100 Rooms.   Business Center of City.

Cor. Jefferson and Center Sts.,

Deadwood	$24 00	Great Bend	$13 25
Elk Point	16 30	Halstead	13 50
Fargo	19 65	Independence	14 50
Jamestown	23 50	Iola	14 50
Montpelier	23 50	Lawrence	13 50
Northwood	20 50	Leavenworth	13 50
Ordway	18 40	Manhattan	13 50
Rapid City	20 50	McPherson	13 50
Salem	20 65	Newton	13 50
Sterling	23 50	Olathe	13 50
Vermillion	16 40	Osage City	13 50
Watertown	18 40	Ottawa	13 90
Yankton	16 50	Princeton	14 25
		Richmond	14 25

Express rates, per 100 lbs., from Phœnix to following offices in

IDAHO.

		Sedgwick	13 50
		Strong City	13 50
		Topeka	13 50
		Valley Center	13 50
Albion	$17 25	Waverly	14 25
Bellevue	17 25	Wichita	13 50
Blackfoot	15 50	Winfield	13 50
Boise City	18 25	Wyandotte	13 50
Caldwell	16 75		
Challis	23 50		

Express rates, per 100 lbs., from Phœnix to following points in

Eagle Rock	15 75	
Franklin	14 25	
Hailey	17 50	

MONTANA.

Ketchum	17 75	
Lewiston	20 00	Anaconda	$18 50
Moscow	17 25	Billings	20 25
Pocatillo	15 25	Bozeman	19 75
Soda Springs	15 50	Butte	18 50
Weiser	16 00	Custer	20 50
		Deer Lodge	18 50
		Dillon	18 25

Express rates, per 100 lbs., from Phœnix to following offices in

		Fort Keogh	21 00
		Garrison	18 75
		Helena	19 75
		Jefferson	19 00

KANSAS.

Arkansas City	$13 50	Marysville	20 25
Atchison	13 50	Miles City	21 00
Burlingame	13 50	Missoula	18 50
Caldwell	13 50	Trout Creek	17 50
Carbondale	13 50	Virginia City	21 00
Chanute	14 50		
Cherryvale	14 50		

Express rates, per 100 lbs., from Phœnix to following offices in

Coffeyville	14 75	
Concordia	14 75	

NEBRASKA.

Dodge City	13 25		
El Dorado	13 50	Ashland	$15 00
Emporia	13 50	Auburn	14 50
Eureka	13 50	Beatrice	14 75
Fredonia	14 75	Bellevue	15 00
Garden City	13 25	Brownville	14 75

Brown House,

THOS. BROWN, Prop'r.

Phœnix, - - - Arizona.

ELEGANTLY FURNISHED ROOMS,

Transient and Permanent.

This new house, situated on the corner of JEFFERSON and PIMA STREETS, is within one block of the City Hall and convenient to the Railroad Depot and business portion of the town. The rooms are commodious, light and airy and furnished throughout in an elegant and tasty manner, with all modern conveniences.

First-Class Patronage Solicited.

JAS. K. BURNETT,

 # Expressman,

WILL DELIVER

TRUNKS, VALISES and Other BAGGAGE

To all parts of town with care and promptness. Will also call for same to be delivered at all outgoing trains.

Passengers Coming into Phœnix

would save time by handing their checks to the Baggage Master on the train, with instructions to deliver their baggage to me; or, they will find me in charge of W., F. & Co's wagon at the Depot.

Orders left at W., F. & Co's Office, in Phœnix, will receive Prompt Attention.

JAS. K. BURNETT.

Central City	$15 25	Los Lunas	$9 75
Columbus	15 25	Manuelito	12 00
Crete	15 00	Nutt	8 00
Dakota	15 25	Rincon	8 25
David City	16 25	San Antonio	9 25
Delvitt	14 75	San Marcial	9 00
Dorchester	15 00	San Miguel	11 25
Dunbar	14 75	Santa Fe	11 00
Endicott	14 75	Separ	7 00
Exeter	15 00	Silver City	8 50
Fairmont	15 00	Socorro	9 25
Falls City	14 25	Stein's Pass	6 25
Fremont	15 25	Wallace	10 50
Grand Island	15 25	Wingate	11 75
Harvard	15 25		
Hastings	15 00		
Inland	15 25		
Juniata	15 25		
Kearney	15 50		
Lincoln	14 75		
McCook	15 75		
Nebraska City	15 00		
Norfolk	15 75		
Omaha	15 00		
Plattsmouth	15 00		
Red Cloud	15 25		
Republican	15 50		
Seward	15 00		
South Bend	15 00		
Syracuse	15 00		
Tecumseh	14 50		
Unadilla	15 00		
Verdon	14 25		
Waverley	15 00		
West Point	16 00		
York	15 00		

Express rates, per 100 lbs., from Phœnix to following offices in

NEW MEXICO.

Albuquerque	$10 25
Bernalillo	10 25
Coolidge	11 75
Deming	7 50
Engle	8 50
Gallup	11 75
Georgetown	11 00
Lake Valley	8 25
Lamy	10 75
Las Cruces	8 50
Las Vegas	11 50
Lordsburg	6 75

Express rates, per 100 lbs., from Phœnix to following offices in

OREGON.

Albany	$11 75
Ashland	10 50
Astoria	11 75
Baker City	14 75
Canyonville	12 50
Corvallis	11 50
Dallas	12 00
Dalles (The)	12 25
East Portland	11 25
Empire City	9 00
Eugene	12 00
Hillsboro	11 50
Jacksonville	11 75
La Grande	14 50
Marshfield	9 00
Oakland	12 00
Oregon City	11 50
Pendleton	13 75
Phœnix	10 75
Portland	11 00
Rosebury	11 75
Salem	11 50
Umatilla	13 25
Union	14 50
Weston	14 25
Yaquina	11 75

Express rates, per 100 lbs., from Phœnix to following offices in

TEXAS.

Albany	$11 75
Austin	12 00
Brenham	12 75

Bryan.	$13 00	Goldendale	$15 00
Calvert	12 75	Kalama	11 50
Cisco	10 50	Palouse Junction.	15 50
Corsicana	11 75	Port Gamble	13 00
Dallas	11 25	Port Ludlow	13 00
Denison	11 50	Port Townsend	13 00
Eagle Pass	10 75	Seattle	12 50
El Paso	7 50	Spokane Falls	16 50
Fort Worth	11 00	Tacoma	12 00
Galveston	12 50	Vancouver	11 50
Hearne	12 25	Walla Walla	14 25
Hempstead	13 00	Wallula Junction	14 25
Houston	12 50	Yakima	16 00
Kaufman	11 75		
La Grange	12 00	*Express rates, per 100 lbs., from Phœnix*	
Luling	11 50	*to following offices in*	
Marfa	9 00		
Morgan	12 00	**WYOMING.**	
Murphysville	9 25	Aspen	$14 00
Plano	12 25	Bryan	14 75
Richmond	12 50	Carbon	16 50
Rosenberg	12 50	Cheyenne	15 00
San Antonio	11 25	Evanston	13 75
Sherman	11 50	Granger	14 50
Spofford Junction	10 50	Green River	15 00
Victoria	13 00	Laramie	15 75
Waco	11 75	Rawlings	16 25
Wacahache	12 50	Rock Creek	16 25
Ysleta	8 00		

Express rates, per 100 lbs., from Phœnix to following offices in

UTAH.

Express rates, per 100 lbs., from Phœnix to following offices in

MEXICO.

Corinne	$13 00	Aguascalientes	$17 50
Frisco	17 25	Celaya	17 50
Kellton	13 00	Chihuahua	11 00
Logan	14 00	El Salto	17 50
Milford	17 00	Ensenada	9 25
Nephi	15 00	Fresnillo	17 25
Ogden	13 00	Guanajuato	17 50
Park City	14 50	Guaymas	7 00
Provo	14 00	Guadalajara	27 50
Salt Lake City	13 75	Hermosillo	6 50
St. George	27 00	Jimenez	12 50
Silver Reef	27 00	Jimulco	14 75
Tintic	15 50	Lagos	17 50
Wahsatch	13 75	Lerdo	14 00
		Magdalena	5 75
Express rates, per 100 lbs., from Phœnix		Mapimi	14 00
to following offices in		Matamoras	14 25
WASHINGTON TERR.		Mazatlan	9 00
Colfax	$16 75	Mexico (City of)	17 50
Dayton	14 50	Orizaba	20 75

Paso del Norte............	$ 8 00
Puebla....................	19 75
Queretaro.................	17 50
San Luis Potosi...........	27 50
San Juan del Rio..........	17 50
Santa Rosalia.............	12 00
Silas.....................	17 50
Vera Cruz.................	22 00
Zacatecas	17 50

*Express rates, per 100 lbs., from Phœnix
to the following*

Cities East of the Missouri River.

Baltimore, Md...	$17 00
Binghampton, N. Y.	18 00
Birmingham, Ala..........	15 00
Boston, Mass.............	17 50
Buffalo, N. Y............	17 25
Burlington, Ia...........	15 00
Cairo, Ills..............	15 50
Chattanooga, Tenn........	17 50
Chicago, Ills............	15 50
Cincinnati, Ohio.........	16 00
Cleveland, Ohio..........	17 00
Columbus, Ohio	16 50
Council Bluffs, Ia.......	14 50
Dayton, Ohio.............	16 25
Detroit, Mich............	16 50
Erie, Pa.................	17 50
Evansville, Ind..........	15 75
Fitchburg, Mass..........	17 50
Fort Wayne, Ind..........	16 25
Harrisburg, Pa...........	17 75
Indianapolis, Ind........	15 75
Kansas City, Mo..........	13 00
London, Can...	17 25
Louisville, Ky.	16 00
Memphis, Tenn............	14 75
Milwaukee, Wis...........	16 00
Montreal, Can............	18 50
Nashville, Tenn.	16 50
New Orleans, La..........	13 00
New York, N. Y...........	17 50
Philadelphia, Pa.........	17 25
Pittsburg, Pa............	16 75
Portland, Me.	17 75
Quebec, Can.	19 20
Quincy, Ill..............	14 50
Richmond, Va.............	18 25
Rochester, N. Y..........	17 50
Rock Island, Ill.	15 00
Salamanca, N. Y..........	17 75

Sandusky, Ohio...........	$17 25
Springfield, Ill.........	15 25
Springfield, Mass........	17 50
Springfield, Ohio........	16 25
St. Louis, Mo............	14 50
St. Joseph, Mo...........	13 00
St. Paul, Minn...........	16 50
Syracuse, N. Y...........	17 50
Toledo, Ohio.............	16 50
Washington, D. C.........	17 00
Wheeling, W. Va..........	16 75
Youngstown, Ohio.........	17 25
Zanesville, Ohio.........	16 75

*Express rates, per 100 lbs., from Phœnix
to following*

FOREIGN COUNTRIES.

Austria..................	$24 50
Belgium..................	26 00
Denmark..................	26 00
England..................	24 50
Finland..................	30 50
France...................	27 50
Germany..................	24 50
Holland..................	26 00
Ireland..................	24 50
Italy....................	27 50
Norway...................	26 00
Poland...................	30 50
Portugal.................	27 50
Russia...................	30 50
Sweden...................	26 00
Switzerland..............	26 50
Turkey	29 50

E. M. MILLS, Proprietor,

PHŒNIX, - - - ARIZONA.

Leading Hotel of Arizona.

CENTRALLY LOCATED,

*Sunny and well Ventilated, Noted for its Excellent Table,
Street Cars pass the House every few minutes,
Free 'Bus from the Depot.*

The Patronage of Tourists, Business Men and
Families Solicited.

ARMY HEADQUARTERS.

E. M. MILLS, - - Manager.

TELEGRAPHIC TARIFFS

FROM

PHŒNIX

TO

LOCAL RATES.	10 Words.	Each Additional Word.
Tempe—Ft. McDowell—Whipple Bks. and Verde...	15c.	and 1c.
Maricopa	25	2
Prescott, via Whipple Bks....................	40	3
Gila Bend, Casa Grande, Sentinel and Texas Hill....	50	4
Tucson and Pantano...........................	65	5

STATE RATES.		
Arizona, New Mexico and Southern California......	75	5
Colorado, Utah, Nevada, West Texas and North Cala.	85	6
British Columbia, Idaho, Kansas, Montana, Wyoming, Nebraska, Oregon, East Texas, Washington Territory	1 00	7
All other points on WESTERN UNION lines	1 25	9

	10 Words.	Each Additional Word.			
Where the Day rate is	65c	and 5c	Night is..	55	and 4
" " "	75	5	"	65	5
" " "	85	6	"	75	5
" " "	1 00	7	"	90	6
" " "	1 25	9	"	1 25	9

IT STILL LEADS!

HIGHLAND CANAL CO.

This new enterprise, now under construction, will open up to settlement 25 sections, or 16,000 acres, of the finest Fruit, Grape and Alfalfa Land to be found in the Salt River Valley. The soil is similar in character to that around Mesa City, a few miles west, which Hon. J. DeBarth Shorb pronounces "the only natural sherry district on this continent."

The Canal now being built will be 22 miles in length, 16 feet wide, and 2½ feet deep, with a carrying capacity of 6,000 inches of water.

JAMES A. BAYARD,
President.

J. F. MEADOR,
Sec'y and Treasurer.

AUSTIN CARRINGTON,
Gen'l Manager.

KELLY & MARLOW,

WHOLESALE AND RETAIL

BUTCHERS

IRVINE BLOCK, WASHINGTON ST.

PHŒNIX, ARIZONA.

1850.   **J. E. WHARTON, M. D.**   1888.

Physician, Surgeon and Accoucheur,

THIRTY-EIGHT YEARS' PRACTICE.

Thirteen Years at N. E. Corner Maricopa and Adams Streets,

PHŒNIX, ARIZONA.

J. M. CREIGHTON,

ARCHITECT,

Office, Porter Block, ...   Phœnix, Arizona.

F. P. TROTT,

Civil Engineer & Surveyor,

PHŒNIX, ARIZONA.

J. W. BLANKENSHIP,

Real Estate and General Auctioneer

Careful attention given to sales of every description.

Constable of Phœnix.

Office, Corner Center and Adams Sts.   *PHŒNIX, ARIZONA.*

MISS KATIE A. BAGLEY,

DRESSMAKER

TEMPE, · · · · · **ARIZONA.**

DEALS ALSO IN

CANDIES, NUTS, FRUITS, STATIONERY AND TOBACCO.

Davis House

TEMPE, ARIZONA.

Everything New and in the Latest Style.

o o o o o o o o o o o o o

Rooms Large and Airy.

Elegant Dining Room.

o o o o o o o o o o o o o

We Employ only White Help.

Table Supplied with all the Delicacies of the Season.

www.ingramcontent.com/pod-product-compliance
Lightning Source LLC
Chambersburg PA
CBHW021533270326
41930CB00008B/1228